T. H. James

The Hare of Inaba

T. H. James

The Hare of Inaba

ISBN/EAN: 9783744708364

Printed in Europe, USA, Canada, Australia, Japan

Cover: Foto ©ninafisch / pixelio.de

More available books at **www.hansebooks.com**

Japanese Fairy Tale Series. No. 11.

THE HARE OF INABA.

*Told to Children
by Mrs. T. H. James.*

Published by the KOBUNSHA, 2, Minami Saegicho, TOKYO.

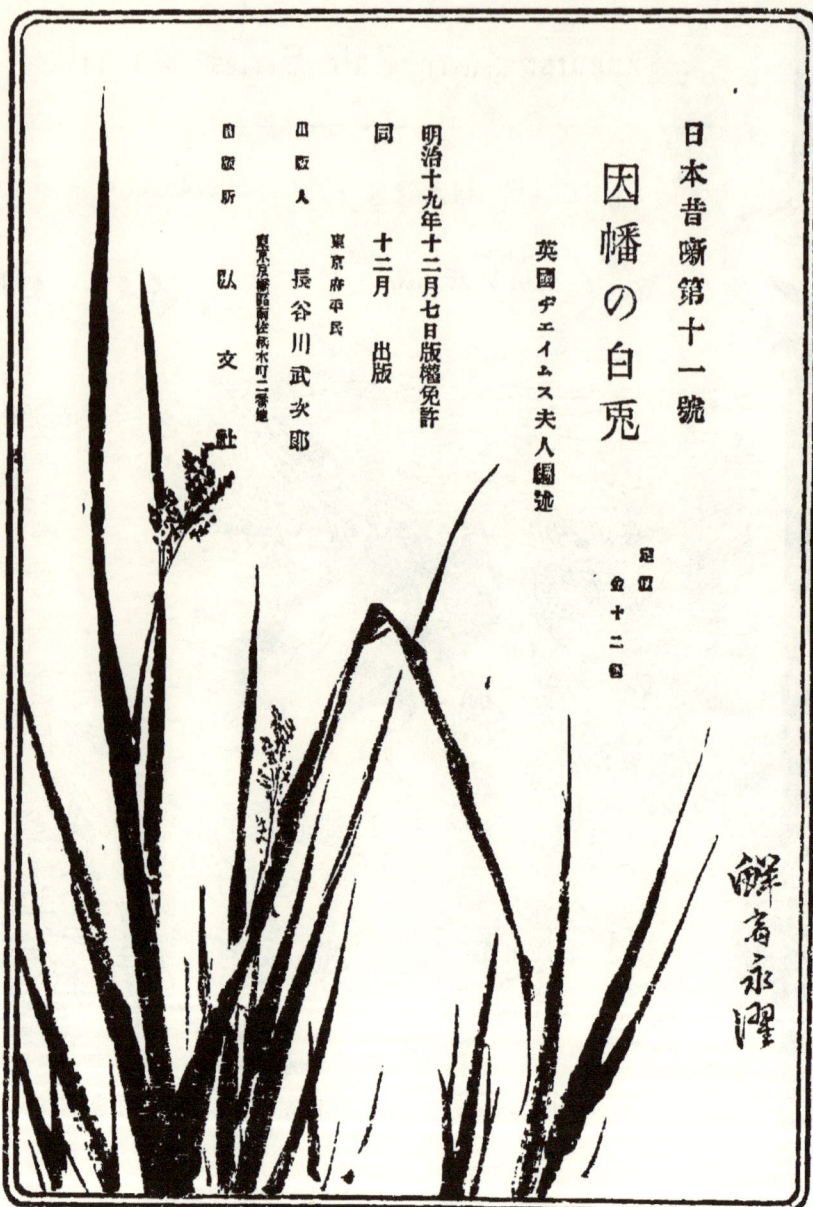

日本昔噺第十一號

因幡の白兎

英國デイムス夫人編述

定價
金十二錢

明治十九年十二月七日版權免許

同　十二月　出版

東京府平民
出版人　長谷川武次郎
東京京橋區南佐柄木町二番地

出版所　弘文社

畫者永濯

THE HARE OF INABA.

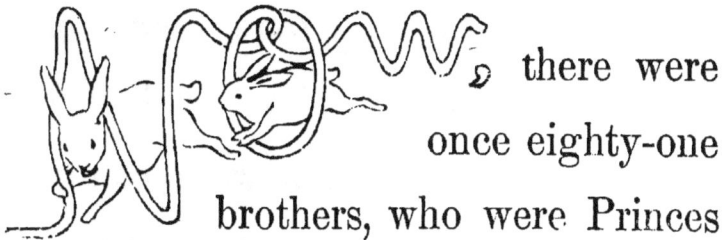

there were once eighty-one brothers, who were Princes in the land. They were all jealous of one another, each one wishing to be King, to rule over the others, and over the whole Kingdom. Besides this, each one wanted to marry the same Princess. She was the Princess of Yakami in Inaba.

At last they made up their minds

that they would go together to Ina_
ba, and each one try to persuade the
Princess to marry him. Although
eighty of these brothers were jealous
of one another, yet they all agreed
in hating, and being unkind to the
eighty-first, who was good and gen-
tle, and did not like their rough, quar-
relsome ways. When they set out
upon their journey, they made the
poor eighty-first brother walk behind
them, and carry the bag, just as if
he had been their servant, although
he was their own brother, and as
much a Prince as any of them all.

By and by, the eighty Princes came to Cape Keta, and there they found a poor hare, with all his fur plucked out, lying down very sick and miserable. The eighty Princes said to the hare,

"We will tell you what you should do.

Go and bathe in the sea water, and
then lie down

on the slope of a high mountain,
and let the wind blow upon you.
That will soon make your fur grow,
we promise you."

So the poor hare believed them,

and went and bathed in the sea, and afterwards lay down in the sun and the wind to dry. But, as the salt water dried, the skin of his body all cracked and split with the sun and the wind, so that he was in terrible pain, and lay there crying, in a much worse state than he was before.

Now the eighty-first brother was a long way behind the others, because he had the luggage to carry, but at last he came up, staggering under the weight of the heavy bag. When he saw the hare he asked,

"Why are you
lying there crying?"
"Oh dear!" said
the hare,

"just stop a moment and I will tell you all my story. I was in the island of Oki, and I wanted to cross over to this land. I didn't know how to get over, but at last I hit upon a plan. I said to the sea crocodiles,

"Let us count how many crocodiles there are in the sea, and how
many hares there are in the land.
And now to begin with the crocodiles. Come, every one of you, and
lie down in a row, across from this
island to Cape Keta, then I will
step upon each one, and count you
as I run across. When I have
finished counting you, we can
count the hares, and then we shall
know whether there are most hares,
or most crocodiles."

The crocodiles came and lay
down in a row. Then I stepped on

them and counted them as I ran across, and was just going to jump on shore, when I laughed and said, "You silly crocodiles, I don't care how many of you there are. I only wanted a bridge to get across by." Oh! why did I boast until I was safe on dry land? For the last crocodile, the one which lay at the very end of the row, seized me, and

plucked off all my fur."

"And serve you right too, for being so tricky." said the eighty-first brother; "however, go on with your story,"

"As I was lying here crying,"

continued the hare, "the eighty Princes who went by before you, told me to bathe in salt water, and lie down in the wind. I did as they told me, but I am ten times worse than before, and my whole body is smarting and sore."

Then the eighty-first brother said to the hare, "Go quickly now to the river, it is quite near. Wash yourself well with the fresh water, then take the pollen of the sedges growing on the river bank, spread it about on the ground, and roll among it; if you do this, your skin will heal, and your fur grow again."

So the hare
did as he
was told;

and this time he was quite cured, and his fur grew thicker than ever. Then the hare said to the eighty-first brother, "As for those eighty Princes, your brothers, they shall not get the Princess of Inaba. Although you carry

the
bag, yet your
Highness shall at last get
both the princess and the country."

Which things came to pass, for the Princess would have nothing to do with those eighty bad brothers, but chose the eighty-first who was kind and good. Then he was made King of the country, and lived happily all his life.